Date Due

BRODART, INC.   Cat. No.

DRUG BUSTERS

The high-tech war on drugs

Photography by Henry Rasmussen

Motorbooks International
Publishers & Wholesalers Inc
Osceola, Wisconsin 54020, USA

First published in 1987 by Motorbooks International Publishers & Wholesalers Inc, PO Box 2, 729 Prospect Avenue, Osceola, WI 54020 USA

Motorbooks International is a certified trademark, registered with the United States Patent Office

Printed and bound in Hong Kong

The information in this book is true and complete to the best of our knowledge. All recommendations are made without any guarantee on the part of the author or publisher, who also disclaim any liability incurred in connection with the use of this data or specific details

Library of Congress Cataloging-in-Publication Data
Rasmussen, Henry
   Drug busters.

   1. Narcotics, Control of—Florida—Pictorial works.
2. Narcotic enforcement agents—Florida—Pictorial
works.   I. Title.
HV5831.F6R37 1987   363.4'5'09759 87-10830
ISBN 0-87938-247-3

Motorbooks International books are also available at discounts in bulk quantity for industrial or sales-promotional use. For details write to Special Sales Manager at the Publisher's address

On the frontispiece: The crew of a Customs speedboat scans the horizon from its vantage point at the edge of the Gulf Stream. An intercept order has just been received, but before the powerful twin engines are brought into action, the captain waits for the appearance of the white-water tail of the suspected speedboat—the element of surprise is crucial.

On the title page: A 41 ft US Coast Guard patrol boat, a vessel that has proven itself to be one of the most versatile workhorses of the fleet. Reasonably fast, sea worthy and incredibly robust, it is as well suited for search and rescue as for chase and seizure.

On this page: A Remington riot-type shotgun gives this Coast Guard officer the kind of authority no one argues with.

Contents

Rewards of a risky business

The drug problem facing our nation is tackled with a new and coordinated vigor these days. All the facets of this battle have their importance, but for the purpose of this book the focus is on the forces responsible for limiting the flow of drugs that continuously erodes our borders. And even the broadest aspect of that focus is too wide for the relatively limited scope of these pages, which are mainly targeted to readers fascinated by the technical aspect. Thus, the focus is not on the organizational structures and the personnel of these drug-fighting forces, but on the equipment they use—the planes, the helicopters, the ships, the speedboats—in short, the drug busters on these pages are not so much the people, as they are the machines.

And while people are indeed running the machines, and while the valor of these people is of extreme importance, and while experience and training and organizational coordination has improved immensely, it is the machines that are going to make the ultimate difference in this war.

Perhaps the most important organizational innovation of the new interdiction efforts has been the creation of the Blue Lightning Strike Force, operating in southern Florida. It includes personnel in six federal agencies, such as Customs and the Coast Guard, as well as in twenty-two local police departments. All are brought together under one command and directed from an operations center in Miami, equipped with the latest in computers and monitoring systems. These systems receive and coordinate information from electronic surveillance gear that includes everything from airborne radar to scanners mounted atop high buildings along the coast and on floating platforms at sea. Under this umbrella command—which can also call on Navy and Air Force units—the individual forces are coordinated into common actions.

So, does it all work? Are there any rewards? Unofficial estimates suggest that about twenty percent of the traffic is intercepted. But perhaps the rewards are best illustrated on an individual level, as depicted by the photograph on this spread, which shows the special agent in charge of Customs operations on Marco Island as he checks one of the 435 bales of marijuana—with a street value of $15 million—caught in a bust the previous night. This crowning act was the result of six weeks of intensive efforts, and a successful operation like this, has an almost euphoric effect on the individuals involved.

On the other side of the coin are the negative rewards of the people who are caught—in the case mentioned, perhaps ten years each in prison for the half-dozen people who operated the fishing boats carrying the marijuana. One of these boats, incredibly enough, was named *Risky Business.*

High-tech eyes in the sky

One of the keys to successful drug interdiction is the ability to discover a plane or vessel as early as possible. To this end, law enforcement agencies monitor the intelligence gathered by the same AWACS (Airborne Warning And Control Systems) planes and TARS (Tethered Aerostat Radar Systems) balloons used to supply information for the nation's early-warnings system. Furthermore, two E-2C spy planes have recently been supplied to the Coast Guard solely for the purpose of discovering and tracking drug runners. The Coast Guard also flies a fleet of planes and helicopters equipped with some of the latest and most effective electronic surveillance systems available. These aircraft crisscross the skies in a pattern of scheduled patrols and, although also employed in search-and-rescue missions as well as in the enforcement of environmental laws, they are on constant watch for vessels and planes suspected of drug smuggling. Customs, in an even more aggressive manner, flies a fleet of unmarked planes equipped with electronic tracking gear so sophisticated its exact specifications are classified.

In this photograph the camera has captured a unit of the Coast Guard fleet of Falcon jets on a reconnaissance mission somewhere between Bimini and Fort Lauderdale. The Mystere-Falcon, which carries a Coast Guard designation of HU-25A Guardian, is a French plane, designed and built by Dassault-Breguet, the same company that produces the famous Mirage fighters. However, the Falcon is powered by two American-made Garrett jet engines which, together with other equipment, makes the craft fifty-six percent American components.

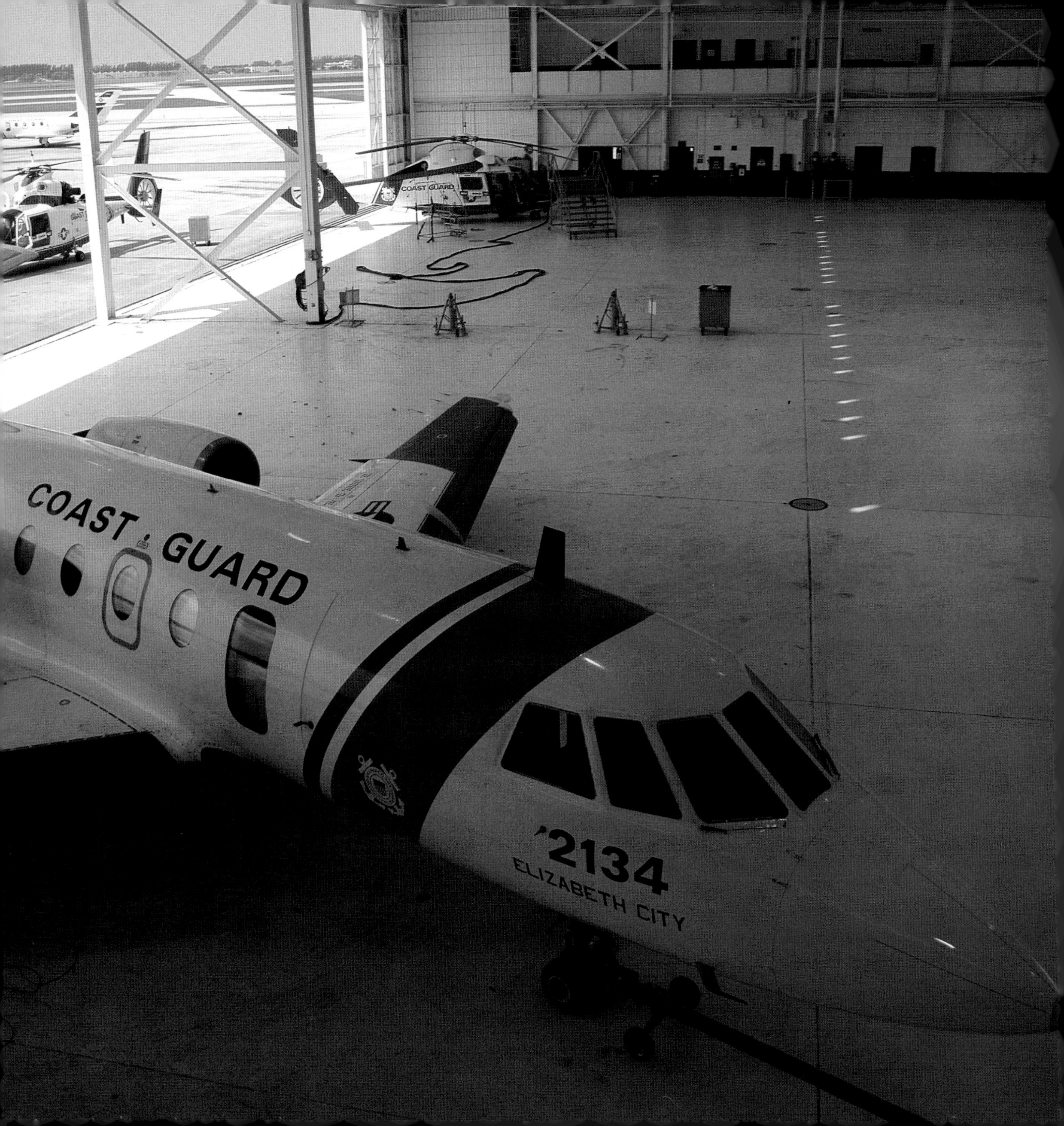
COAST GUARD
COAST GUARD
'2134
ELIZABETH CITY

Delivery of the Coast Guard Falcons began early in 1982, and by the end of the following year, all forty-one units contracted for had been delivered. The Falcons operate out of nine stations around the nation, with the largest number counting Air Station Miami as their homebase. Seen to the left, the *Elizabeth City* in its hangar at the base, which is located in Opa-Locka. The Falcon has a 53 ft wingspan, is 56 ft long, and stands 17 ft tall. Operating weight, with a crew of five, is about 21,000 lb.

One of the six Falcons stationed at Opa-Locka, the *Miami,* sports a curious auxiliary pod, seen immediately ahead of the wing in the picture above. This contains elements of the Aireye system which, among other components, consists of the SLAR (Side Looking Airborne Radar). This unit, coupled to a steerable TV camera with laser illumination, the AGTV (Active Gated TV), is capable of scanning and photographing a 100-mile-wide path below the plane, in all kinds of weather, day or night. Maximum cruising speed for the Falcon is 460 knots, or 530 mph. Range is 2,600 miles, or approximately four hours.

Next page
The new Coast Guard helicopter, carrying a Coast Guard designation of HH-65A, is like the Falcon of French origin, designed and manufactured by Aerospatiale. The two jet engines, however, are Avco Lycomings, and together with the communications and navigation equipment, which is manufactured by Rockwell Collins, they add up to a sixty-percent American component content. The Coast Guard received its first Dolphin late in 1984. Deliveries will continue until 1988, when the total order of ninety-nine units will have been completed.

In the picture on this spread, a Dolpin is being prepared for take-off by its three-man crew, which consists of the pilot, co-pilot and aircrewman, the latter responsible for operating the rescue hoist. The craft has a 38-ft-long fuselage. The overall height is 13 ft. The weight, with equipment, is about 6,000 lb. Much of the fuselage is made from a superlight composite material. Fiberglas and Kevlar are used wherever possible for further weight reduction. The rotors measure 39 ft in diameter. Never-exceed speed is 175 knots, or 200 mph. Maximum cruising speed is 140 knots, or 160 mph. Range is somewhat shorter than that of the Falcon, approximately three hours.

Shown in the photograph to the left, a close-up side view of the Dolphin with its engine cover removed. The two jet engines produce 740 shp (horsepower measured at the shaft) each. The main rotor blades are built around carbon-fiber spars, which in turn are covered with a carbonfiber skin. The leading edges are made from Fiberglas, with a sheathing of stainless steel providing the final touch. The blades are designed to disintegrate upon contact with any substantial object, such as the waves of the ocean.

The Coast Guard is a very professional organization, functioning much like the Air Force and the Navy, with chains of command and rigorous rules and regulations. Safety is, of course, one of the foremost concerns. Pictured above is the type of helmet worn by helicopter pilots and crew. Ear phones are built in, with a spiral cord connecting to outlets in the cabin for internal communication. Both the Falcon and the Dolphin are unarmed, as are their pilots and crews. These craft are usually not involved in the actual capture of suspects, but are used in the tracking and chasing phases. On a recent occasion, however, a Dolphin held a speedboat at bay using its rotor blast, until surface vessels arrived to perform the final act.

Previous page
The mean visage in the photograph on the previous spread, belongs to one of the fleet of unmarked Piper Cheyennes operated by Customs. As the long snout reveals, this is no ordinary aircraft. In Customs lingo, this plane is a CHET (Customs High Endurance Tracker). The nose hides a radar unit, while the protrusion under the fuselage houses the eye of a classified infrared surveillance system. Once the radar is locked onto the target, the infrared system stays on it, producing a detailed black and white image on a screen. This picture is in turn recorded by a TV camera, thus providing accurate data of an event as well as evidence for use in an eventual trial. The Customs Cheyennes are fitted with additional fuel tanks that allow them to stay aloft as long as seven hours. Wingspan is 48 ft, length 43 ft, height 15 ft. Empty weight is about 7,000 lb. The two 720 shp Pratt & Whitney turboprop engines give the Cheyenne a maximum cruising speed of 315 knots, or 365 mph, which is enough to keep pace with a DC-6, a plane commonly used for transporting contraband.

Pictured on this spread, one of the Cessna Citations operated by Customs. It is also a CHET, equipped with the same systems as the Piper Cheyenne. The Citation is slightly larger and faster, however. Wingspan is 52 ft, length 47 ft, height 15 ft. Empty weight is 8,000 lb. The two Pratt & Whitney jet engines produce a maximum cruising speed of 400 knots, or 460 mph. The CHETs are responding to alerts from intelligence obtained by AWACS and other sources. Their mission is to track down a suspected plane and take up a position behind it. From this vantage point they can observe and record activities such as air drops. The units operate out of Homestead Air Force Base, just south of Miami. Like the Coast Guard, Customs is a highly professional organization. However, its air branch resembles an independent commando unit—with less emphasis on formality and dress code, for instance—rather than a conventional military squad. However, readiness—stand-by aircraft must be airborne eight minutes after alert—is very high, as is combat morale.

Longest arms of the law

The surveillance and tracking duties performed by the Customs CHETs pertain mainly to activities in the air, and focus on aircraft that take off from, for instance, Colombia, and make their way across the Mexican Gulf to a rendezvous with a ship, or to a strip or drop point on one of the numerous islands and keys in the Bahamian archipelago, or on the Florida mainland itself. But for far-reaching reconnaissance at sea, drug enforcement agencies rely on the Coast Guard and its high-endurance cutters. Staying out for a month at a time, the mission of these ships is to patrol the three passages that all sea traffic must pass on its way north: the Yucatan Channel, between Mexico and Cuba; the Windward Pass, between Cuba and Haiti; and the Mona Channel, between the Dominican Republic and Puerto Rico. Using sophisticated radar, as well as other visual surveillance methods, they scan virtually every vessel that comes through. Their visual reconnaissance capabilities are further extended by the use of the Dolphin helicopter, which is carried aboard.

Pictured here is one of the high-endurance vessels in the Coast Guard fleet, the brand-new cutter *Seneca*. With its overall length of 270 ft, this vessel is only out-classed by the 378 ft version. As shown here, the *Seneca* is anchored in the waters off Miami Beach, with its seductive shades of blue and green, and photographed from the Dolphin helicopter that is to be deployed on board for the voyage to the Yucatan Channel.

The scene to the left shows the view from the fast-approaching Dolphin. The helmet and Nomex suit belong to the pilot, who occupies the right seat. The co-pilot, consequently, occupies the left seat. The craft can be operated from either of these positions. The aircrewman occupies a seat immediately behind the two pilots. Using a lever, he can move his chair sideways on a rail, alternating between the two doors located on each side of the craft. The photographer was strapped into the harness normally used by the aircrewman when he operates the hoist; the picture could therefore be snapped from outside the helicopter.

In the photograph above, taken from the *Seneca* and with a telephoto lens, the Dolphin is seen approaching the ship, while the white skyline of Miami Beach wavers unsteadily at the horizon. Notice the protrusion on the left side of the helicopter. This is the location of the hoist mechanism. A rescue basket is permanently carried aboard the aircraft. The Dolphin has a very advanced computerized flight management system. Its state-of-the-art communication and navigation features include a system that, at the pilot's direction, will bring the craft to a stable hover 50 ft above a selected object. This is an innovative safety feature, and of special importance in darkness and bad weather.

The photograph on the previous spread captures the *Seneca* as it appears from the rapidly closing Dolphin. The vessel has a displacement of 1,730 tons, and a maximum speed of 20 knots. It has a crew of 103, whereof fourteen are officers. It was built in 1986. The *Seneca* is so new that this occasion marks the first time it is making its deck available for a helicopter landing. Special instructors are on board to supervise and certify the crew.

The scene on this spread shows the interior of the Dolphin helicopter. The photograph was snapped from the passenger seat, which is located at the very end of the cabin. Although this seat is no more than a cushion on the floor, it is equipped with a five-point restraint, as are all seats on the craft. Safety awareness is acute—even the passenger has to don helmet and Nomex fire-retardant suit. The red cylinder is a flotation element mounted on the basket. A portion of its steel-tube skeleton is visible in the foreground.

Again photographed from the hang-out position afforded by the harness, the scene to the left records the action while the pilot attempts to line up his craft with the pad on the ship—not an easy task when one considers the continuous pitching of the vessel. Notice that each side of the pad is edged by a safety net, since there can be no railings in this section of the ship. Also visible from this angle is the hangar provided for the protection of the Dolphin when it is stored on deck. The hangar doors are marked by two vertical black lines. One half of the hangar fits into the other, and can be moved out to create the full length necessary to enclose all of the helicopter.

Since it is very difficult for the pilot to judge the continuously changing angle and distance to the deck, visual guidance is provided by a flag man—or, as in this case, by a flag woman—aboard the ship. In the picture above, the flag woman, displaying a red flag, indicates that the deck is not clear for landing. During a clear approach, a green flag is displayed, and both arms are stretched out to indicate height and angle. The arms are lowered gradually in a downward motion to indicate the closing gap between landing gear and pad. At the appropriate moment, preferably when the ship is in a down pitch, the arms are lowered in a quick move, urging the pilot to set down. When contact is made, the arms are crossed in rapid, horizontal motions.

The photograph on this spread provides yet another angle of the intricate maneuvering required to land the helicopter on the ship. It also affords an excellent view of the Dolphin itself, from the four rotor blades; the hoisting mechanism with its hook clearly visible; the open loading door, which slides backward—the pilots have their own doors; to the nose dome, which houses the radar system; and the landing gear, which is fully retractable. Under emergency conditions, when the seas are too heavy to allow landing, the helicopter can be refueled through a hose brought up to the craft with the help of the hoist. Should the helicopter end up in the waves, inflatable flotation bags will keep the craft afloat, leaving the crew time for evacuation and, hopefully, for the salvaging of the craft itself.

Next page
Immediately upon contact with the deck, a team of four agile sailors rush forward to the helicopter, bent low to avoid the still spinning rotors. Their task is to tie down the craft, which could otherwise pitch over and slide off the deck. These sailors work quickly, in practiced synchronization, and are in and out in less than half a minute. In the photograph on the following spread, the tiedown straps have just been removed in a reverse maneuver, readying the helicopter for take-off. Two of the sailors have already disappeared out of sight. Their head gear, although they seem to feature ear phones for radio contact, are simply protection from the noise which, in the case of the Dolphin, is very characteristic, with a whining, high-pitched note.

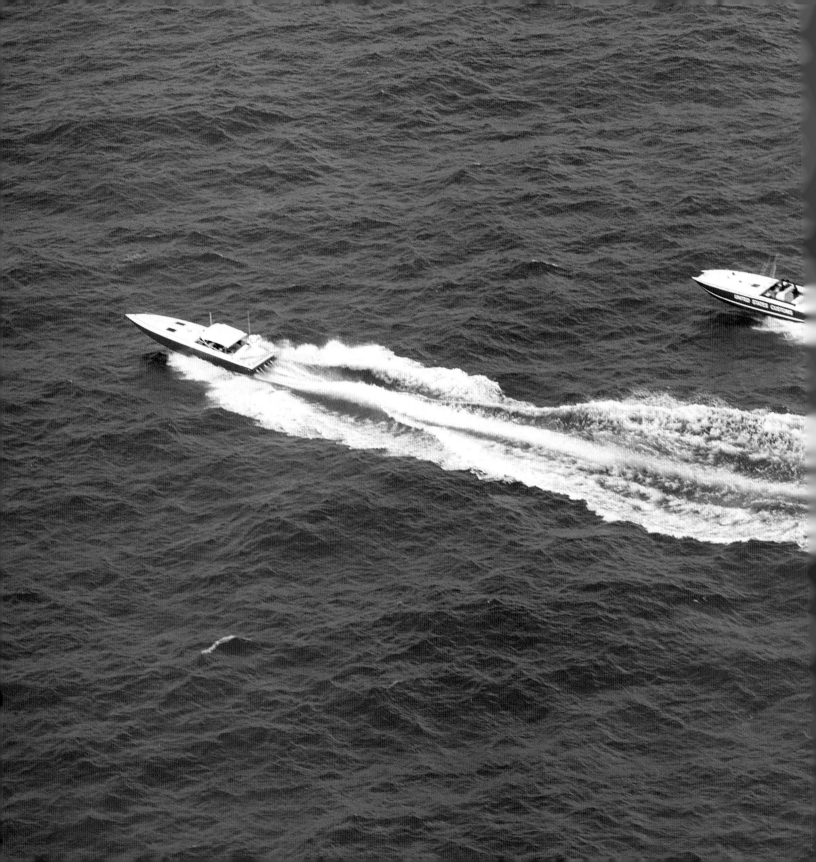

Go-fasts of the good guys

Since the high level of sophistication of the new electronic surveillance systems set up by the drug enforcement authorities has made it virtually suicidal to try to fly directly into the south Florida mainland, the classic method of running speedboats across from, for instance, Bimini in the Bahamas, has again become in vogue among smugglers. The speedboats used in these crossings, commonly referred to as go-fasts—long, sleek, multi-engined creations—have become as fast as rockets. The most potent can reach a top speed of 80 mph, if the conditions are right—that is, if the seas are smooth. The ideal conditions are found during a calm night without a moon. But that is when the go-fasts of the good guys are out there in numbers as well. And their machines have also become more sophisticated—to the point where a world champion speedboat designer has been hired to perform his magic. Thus, in addition to a war on drugs, there is also an unofficial technical development war being fought out there on those seemingly innocent vacation-paradise seas.

These are the tell-tale signs all drug busters are looking for—those long, foaming white-water wakes of go-fasts. Drug runners attempting to do their crossing in full daylight—creating a scene like this—are obviously candidates for having their heads examined. Still, there are those who try. However, the pair pictured here is not out on illegal business—these are two of the latest Customs go-fasts on a reconnaissance mission.

Pictured on this spread, two of the most awesome drug busters in the business. In the air, a Black Hawk helicopter. On the waves, a Blue Thunder speedboat. Both are deployed by Customs. The Blue Thunder, of which about a dozen have been built, was designed by Don Aronow, a former world champion power boat racer. The extremely broad deck of the Blue Thunder, as shown in this picture, is due to its twin-hull design, which gives better stability in high seas. Twin Mercury, 460 cc gasoline engines, located inboard, produce 400 hp each, and a top speed of well over 60 mph. This may not seem enough, considering the 80 mph capability of some of the fastest boats run by the bad guys, but these are generally smaller boats, and have to slow down considerably in rough sea. However, just to be sure, and just to even the odds further—and perhaps finally to outperform the bad guys—the Blue Thunder 400 hp engines are now being replaced by 575 hp units.

Next page
On the following spread, a sea-level shot of the Blue Thunder. Here, all of its 39 ft sleekness passes the camera in a spray of speed and ferocious fury. Although most impressive and authoritative, the thundering sound of the twin Mercurys can be a disadvantage—the whereabouts of the Blue Thunder may be easily detected by the bad guys, whose most clever efforts now include exhaust systems that exit under water, for quieter operation. A closer look at the bow of the Blue Thunder reveals its twin-hull design. This feature, as already mentioned, improves stability, and also gives incredibly impressive maneuverability. It is a most exhilarating experience to be a passenger on the Blue Thunder while it, at high speed, makes a full turn within its own radius. While the g-force is not quite on the level of that of a race car or a fighter plane, it is enough to take your breath away.

The photographs on these pages are taken from a Customs Huey helicopter, flying parallel to the boats, and attempting to coordinate its speed with theirs. The boats jump and bounce like playful whales, and focusing is difficult. Pictured to the left, the chunky Blue Thunder. As can be seen, it has an impressive complement of antennas— voice-privacy radios with often-changed frequencies are of course found on board, as is a transponder that automatically signals the location of the boat to the radar-monitoring operations center.

Pictured above, another Customs go-fast. This is one of a recently acquired fleet of Chris Craft Stingers. These boats are of single-hull construction, and consequently considerably sleeker than the Blue Thunders. They measure 39 ft from bow to stern. Meant to operate mainly in waters closer to the coastline, the Stingers are as fast as their bigger counterparts, but are more sensitive to sea conditions. As a rule, the go-fast has a crew of three, with the captain handling the controls—and always staying with the craft—leaving his two colleagues to the tasks of the boarding.

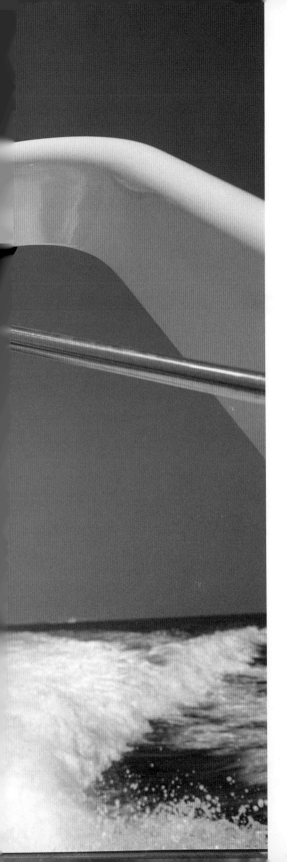

The Chris Craft Stingers are equipped with the same voice-privacy radios and transponder systems found on the Blue Thunders, but in addition the Stingers sport Raytheon radar units. These are mounted on the roll bar. Additional equipment mounted in this area includes a blue flashing light, a loud speaker, and an extremely powerful spotlight. For operation during the dark hours, the crew is equipped with night-vision goggles. These are so efficient that it is possible to read a newspaper in the darkest of nights, and they make that typical white wake created by the go-fasts easy to spot.

Next page
The scene on the following spread shows a Stinger and its crew in action. A vessel fitting one of the profiles of a typical drug runner—in this case, a fishing boat of Bahamian registry—was observed as it neared Miami. Due to the heavy seas off the coast, the captain of the suspected vessel was told to steer his boat inside one of the channels leading to the harbor, where the boarding could safely take place. After a thorough search, including the implementation of "space accountability"—where the volume of visible space is added up and compared with the exterior measurements, to reveal possible hidden compartments— no contraband was found. However, a check with operations center and its all-knowing computer revealed that one of the crew members was sought for previous currency violations.

Every shift begins with a certain maintenance routine. In the photograph to the left, algae are removed from the trim tabs, and the dip sticks are checked for their oil levels. More serious maintenance, such as tuning and engine overhaul, is contracted to outside companies. Customs officers are required to wear the organization's dark blue uniforms, including a cap. A patch on the shirt, an emblem on the cap, and US Customs printed in large letters on the windbreaker leaves no doubt as to their authority.

The Chris Craft Stinger, like the Blue Thunder, is powered by a potent pair of gasoline-operated Mercurys, mounted inboard. The curving twin sets of exhaust pipes—open except for short baffles at the stern—and the round air cleaners, can be seen in the picture above. The Coast Guard has recently also contracted for a fleet of speed boats. However, these are to be powered by diesel engines. Customs officers prefer the quicker response and higher performance of the gasoline version, but admit that they have to contend with its somewhat lower level of reliability.

Captured at speed in the photograph on this spread, the captain of a Stinger, attentively at the controls of his zooming craft. This is not a mere demonstration for the benefit of the photographer—who by the way has a hard time trying to hold onto both camera and safety handle, since the sea is not as placid as the horizon line seems to indicate. This is the beginning of a chase that starts outside Government's Cut, just south of Miami Beach, and ends near Bal Harbor, far to the north. A spot on the radar in the operations center has been discovered to be moving in a westerly direction at a speed in excess of 35 knots. The direction indicates a straight line from Bimini. The Stinger is alerted, and immediately takes off with both engines roaring at 4200 rpm and the speedometer needle pinned down just past the 40 knot mark.

Next page
The Stinger is soon joined in the chase by a sister boat, and the two of them catch up with the suspected vessel just as it enters Biscayne Bay. The bay, with its calm water, separates the mainland from the narrow key that serves as a foundation for the hotel cities of Bal Harbor, Surfside and Miami Beach. In the photograph on the following page, the second Stinger is close on the heels of the speedboat and has ordered it, via the loudspeaker, to slow down for boarding. No contraband is visible on deck, but this does not mean that the boat is clean. Both Stingers have a crew member out on the stern, standing ready with tie-down ropes. Their weapons are clearly visible. Although smugglers caught in the act seldom choose to shoot it out with their captors—they instead prefer to ram their way to freedom—it never hurts to be on the safe side.

51

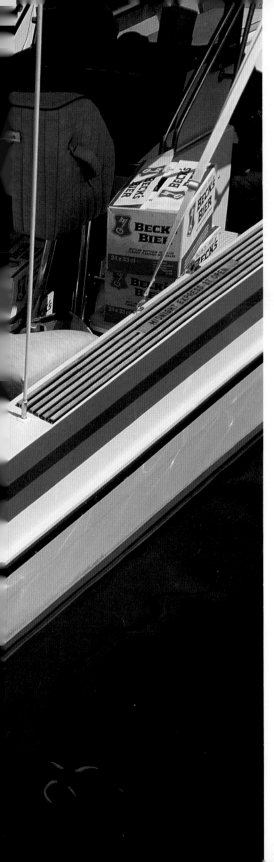

Previous page

In the picture on the previous page the suspected vessel has been boarded and the Customs officers have begun their search for hidden contraband. Even residue found on the floor of the boat can be enough to get the suspects in trouble. This craft is of the type commonly used by drug smugglers. Its open deck is well suited for a bulky load of marijuana bales, allowing rapid on and off loading, as well as ample storage space. Every bag, sack and box is searched carefully, as is every space, compartment and cavity. The boat is found to have exceptionally sophisticated communications gear, far beyond what an average sports fisherman would need. The serial numbers of these components, as well as frequencies, are recorded.

Shown here, a Customs officer on the job. A screwdriver allows access to sealed compartments—compartments that could very well hide contraband. In addition to the open deck, the gleaming row of four outboard Mercurys is further indication of the less-than-pure purpose of this boat. With a collective power of more than 800 horses, the performance is far beyond the needs of the weekend boater. The crew does admit to having made a round trip to Bimini—for the fun of it. But it is questionable fun in the very heavy seas of the day. In addition, the gas alone would have cost $200-300. Had the crew lied about the Bimini visit, the Customs officers would have known anyway: The bottles of beer on board are transparent, the way they are sold on Bimini; this particular brand is only marketed in dark bottles in the United States. In the end, no contraband is found. Was it a test run? Will it be different the next time around?

The photographs on this spread provide unique glimpses of Customs fashion. Pictured above, the ankle holster worn by a Stinger captain, complete with its .38 caliber Smith & Wesson Model 60 Chiefs Special. Every Customs officer is required to carry at least one handgun at all time. Some carry two. A few carry three. The shoes are part of the uniform, and are of the type usually worn by sailors. Rubber soles provide adhesion on slippery deck surfaces, at moments when balance and agility are of the utmost importance.

Pictured to the right, this Customs officer prefers another method of carrying the weapon, the shoulder holster. It holds a Smith & Wesson Model 686, which has a three-inch barrel and is a special L-frame issue for Customs. Within the organization it is referred to as the CS1 (Customs Service 1). It shoots a .357 Magnum round. While the uniform is required dress, there is no regulation regarding additional clothing worn for weather protection. A Harvard sweater adds a certain touch of class.

Definitive drug buster

When it comes to sheer awesomeness, in appearance as well as pure effectiveness of performance, there is no other piece of equipment in the drug enforcement arsenal that can measure up to the Black Hawk helicopter. The very existence of these monsters illustrates the determined attitude and ferocious combat spirit of the Customs Service. The Black Hawk was originally conceived by the military as a transport helicopter. Its mission was to ferry combat troops into hostile territory. As such it is itself heavily armed, capable of carrying both rockets and missiles. Although the Black Hawks used as drug busters are unarmed, they do carry commando-style drug enforcement agents, who themselves are equipped with whatever it takes—automatic rifles, shotguns, handguns, even knives. And these men do know how to use their equipment—even if most of the time only for intimidation. As a drug buster, the mission of the Black Hawk is the administration of the final blow, that of physically catching the criminal and his contraband.

The photograph on this spread illustrates the intimidating appearance of the Black Hawk helicopter. The units in service with the Customs Service are all painted black—not a pretty, shiny black, with elegant pin striping, but a utilitarian, matt black. All it is meant to do is to make the big bird absolutely invisible at night—a time when the Black Hawk is most active.

Previous page

The photograph on the previous spread pictures one of the two Black Hawks stationed at the Customs base at Homestead. The Black Hawk is manufactured by Sikorsky, whose main facilities are located in Stratford and Bridgeport, Connecticut. The Black Hawk prototype made its maiden flight in 1974; the first production unit took to the air in 1978. Deliveries to the Army commenced in 1981. Three years later, 500 units had been delivered. The Black Hawk now serves with, among many other Army branches, the 101st and 82nd Airborne divisions. Overall length of the fuselage is 50 ft. Rotor diameter is 54 ft. Height is 12 ft. Empty weight is in excess of 10,000 lb. However, in the form seen here, the weight of the awesome bird is considerably higher. In fact, special concrete foundations had to be constructed for the Black Hawks before they could begin to operate out of their base at Homestead.

The photograph on this spread reveals one of the reasons for the increased weight of the drug buster Black Hawk. While the standard version has a cabin capable of accommodating an eleven-man infantry squad and its equipment, the Customs version has only room for four passengers. And these passengers have very little elbow room indeed, for the main cabin space is occupied by a gigantic fuel tank. In this picture, the thirsty bird gets a refueling immediately after returning from a mission. The additional fuel enables the Black Hawk to stay in the air for as long as six hours. This high-endurance capability is often of vital importance—a recent mission began over the Gulf of Mexico, and ended somewhere in Virginia.

I ♥ MY BLACK HAWK

POLICE

The scene on this spread is enough to make the uninitiated dizzy! It seems every inch of the Black Hawk cockpit is occupied by instruments and gauges and knobs and switches. There is barely room for the pilot and co-pilot, who occupy armor-plated seats. It takes a certain kind of man to master this confusing array of technology, in the darkness of night and under circumstances when the adrenalin plays havoc with the senses. Special men indeed. And Customs knows how to attract these men. Nicknames such as Mad Dog perfectly describe daring pilots who have been known to jam the landing gear through the windshield of fleeing drug runner's cars, thus preventing their escape. These men truly have more than a paycheck stake in their work.

Next page
Pictured on the next page, a Black Hawk captured during a daylight mission above the shallow waters just south of Miami. Notice the number of busts indicated by the rows of leaves painted on the fuselage, immediately below the pilot's window—green leaves for marijuana busts. white leaves for cocaine busts. The white police script was added recently, when a particular incident made it clear that proper identification was a necessity. Upon the sudden appearance of the menacing-looking Black Hawk, it is imperative that the bad guys immediately realize that it indeed is the police, and not a rival gang about to interfere with their activities. Drug enforcement agents understandably do not relish the thought of being caught in a deadly crossfire between competing drug smugglers.

A frontal view of the Black Hawk, with its menacing look of a prehistoric monster. The awesome power of this potent flying machine comes from two General Electric turboshaft engines, producing as much as 1,560 shp each. Maximum level speed is 160 knots, or 185 mph. Maximum cruising speed is 145 knots, or 165 mph. One pilot quoted a maximum speed of 180 knots—but that was with the throttle wide open and during a slight dive. Should it be necessary, the helicopter can operate on just one engine, in which case the maximum speed is 105 knots, or 120 mph. Vertical rate of climb is 450 ft/min. Hovering ceiling is about 10,000 ft. In this picture, the Black Hawk pilot has turned on its superbright floodlight.

Next page
The scene on the next spread depicts the Black Hawk upon return from an assignment. A recent example of a successful mission provides a glimpse of how well the combination of a Customs CHET and a Black Hawk works. A light plane had been picked up by mission control radar. It had not filed a flight plan, and was flying without lights. The CHET took to the air and, without being noticed, positioned itself on the plane's tail. With the infrared surveillance gear locked onto the small plane, the CHET had a perfectly clear picture of the suspected smuggler, in spite of the total darkness. At the appropriate time, the Black Hawk was notified, and joined the chase when the smuggler landed in a field. As the helicopter turned on its floodlights and touched down, the pilot of the small plane abandoned his craft and fled into the dense forest that surrounded the field. The CHET continued its surveillance and could, thanks to its heat-sensitive scanner, follow the pilot on the screen. There was no escape because the agents from the Black Hawk, now in hot pursuit, could be directed to the exact spot where the man was hiding.

These two photographs offer unique close-up views of the uniforms and weapons worn by the drug enforcement agents aboard the Black Hawk helicopters. To the left, one of the agents displays his choice of arm, a Heckler & Koch HK33E automatic rifle with telescopic stock, manufactured in West Germany. Cyclic rate is 600 rpm. The HK33 is a robust and reliable weapon, and very controllable when fired in the fully automatic mode. Here the largest clip available, which holds forty rounds, gives an extra edge. Also, as in Vietnam combat, the agent has taped together two clips, which gives him easy access to another forty rounds.

The close-up above shows another choice of weapon, in addition to an automatic rifle. Pictured here is a 9 mm Parabellum Smith & Wesson Model 469 double-action automatic pistol. This outstanding unit is a cut-down version of the Model 459, which in turn was a development of the Model 39—one of the all-time best and most reliable combat handguns. With its clip capacity of twelve rounds, the 469 has a definite advantage over revolvers, which hold six rounds, and most other automatic pistols, which normally hold eight. The holster used by the agent in this picture is very small, and allows the quickest possible draw of the weapon.

Crisscrossing combat zones

The Coast Guard already has its hands full with the multitude of duties and services it offers—from simple safety inspections of your average pleasure boat to elaborate rescue missions at sea. The organization is also a force to reckon with when it comes to drug busting. The Coast Guard possesses an impressive fleet of vessels that crisscross the waters off the south Florida coast on a regular basis. These waters are not only some of the world's busiest from the viewpoint of pleasure boating, but have become veritable combat zones in the war between the drug smugglers and the agencies that enforce the law. And the cutters and patrol boats of the Coast Guard are right in the thick of it. As a result of the Reagan Administration's declared war on drugs, the activities of the Coast Guard are now focused to a larger degree than ever before on catching the smugglers.

The *Manitou,* pictured at Base Miami Beach, represents the newest type of vessel in the Coast Guard fleet. The type is referred to as the Island Class and falls into the medium endurance category. The *Manitou* is 110 ft long, has a displacement of 140 tons, a maximum speed of 26 knots, and a range of about 1,800 nautical miles. It is powered by two Taxman Balenta diesels, producing 1,600 hp each. The *Manitou* sails with two officers and two petty officers on board, and a crew of twelve. It was built in Lockport, Louisiana.

To the left, the *Cape Gull,* which is somewhat larger than the *Point Barnes,* with its displacement of 105 tons, and length of 95 ft. This vessel also falls into the medium-size patrol boat category. Power comes from two General Motors diesel engines, each producing 1,200 hp. Maximum speed is 23 knots. Economical cruising speed is 11 knots. Cruising speed is 18 knots. This type of cutter holds a crew of fourteen, including one officer. The *Cape Gull* was built in 1953, at the Coast Guard's own shipyards located in Curtis Bay, just outside Baltimore. Maryland.

Above, the *Point Barnes.* This vessel represents the large fleet of medium-size patrol boats found in the Coast Guard arsenal. The type is equipped for missions lasting about a week. The *Point Barnes* measures 82 ft, has a displacement of sixty-nine tons, and a maximum speed of 23 knots—a pace that can only be maintained for a couple of hours. The cruising speed is about 15 knots. Power comes from two Cummins diesels, each producing 900 hp. The vessel was built in 1970, in Baltimore, Maryland.

This photograph was taken from the bridge of a medium-size Coast Guard patrol boat. It shows three of its crew members in the process of preparing for the small boat to be hoisted on board. The inflatable, rigid-hull, rubber-type small boat is used for boardings as well as for chase and reconnaissance missions. Thanks to its flat bottom, it is especially useful in shallow waters, of which there is plenty among the numerous islands and keys in the area, with its reefs and mangroves. The small boat measures 13 ft in length, and is powered by a Johnson outboard. It usually holds four occupants, but will carry a maximum of six. It can reach a top speed of about 20 knots. When not in use, the small boat is stored on deck.

Next page
Seen on the next spread, the impressive defense capability of a medium-size Coast Guard cutter. The type of vessel featured here has one unit mounted on each side of the deck, just ahead of the bridge. The weapon is a real classic—the .50 caliber M-2 Browning Heavy Barrel machine gun, which was the dependable workhorse of many a World War II battle. It shoots 300 rounds per minute, but firing usually takes place in bursts of three to five rounds at the time. Every fifth round is a tracer, which, with its orange ball of fire, helps the gunner zero in on his target. The magazine holds 100 rounds. A loader makes sure the ammunition belt is running smoothly. The sturdy tripod mounting eliminates any recoil. This particular gun is equipped with an armored shield, which gives the gunner protection in addition to the helmet and flak jacket.

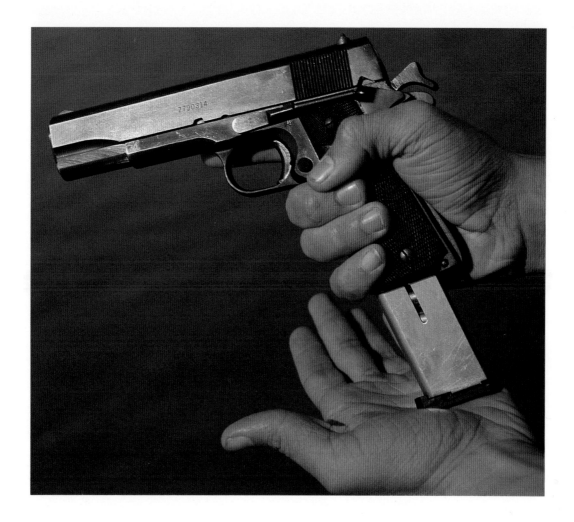

While the airmen of the Coast Guard are not armed, the seamen are—and adequately so. The two photographs on this spread represent standard Coast Guard issue in the form of an M-16A1 automatic rifle, to the left, and an M-1911A1 automatic pistol, above. The 5.56 mm M-16, which saw action in Vietnam, and is the standard rifle of the US Army, is manufactured by Colt. The low weight of the weapon, just 6 lb 5 oz, is a much appreciated feature. The Coast Guard uses it with the largest, thirty-round, banana clip. The cyclic rate is 800 rpm.

The M-1911A1 is a real old-timer, and it is something of a contradiction that this weapon is still in use, considering the sophistication found in other areas of the armament industry. But the good old workhorse can still be trusted. The .45 caliber M-1911 originates from a design by John Browning, and was developed just before the turn of the century. An improved version was adopted by the US Army in 1911, and a further improved version is still standard issue. By the end of World War II, as many as two and a half million units had been manufactured, mainly by Colt, but also by Remington and others. The clip holds six cartridges.

The photograph on this spread was snapped from the deck of one of the Coast Guard's 41 ft boats, of which more than a dozen are operating in the waters off the coast of southern Florida. These boats, although always referred to as "Forty-one-footers," do carry a Coast Guard designation of UTB, which stands for Utility Boat. Its deck and hull are manufactured from aluminum, while the cabin is made from reinforced Fiberglas. The Forty-one-footers are built at the Coast Guard shipyards in Curtis Bay, Maryland. In this picture, a suspicious-looking freighter is getting a thorough looking-over while passing the Government's Cut approach to Miami harbor. Notice the tow line at the bottom of the picture.

Next page
The scene on the next page captures the tense atmosphere inside the cabin of a Forty-one-footer engaged in a chase—the tenseness is caused by the fact that the seas are unruly and the waves have to be negotiated with a certain amount of care. Since the surveillance activities in the waters between Miami and Bimini have been intensified, the drug smugglers have adapted to the new situation by sometimes using less conspicuous vessels than the go-fasts; sailboats are often found to be carrying contraband. Here, a pair of suspicious sails have been spotted on the horizon, and the captain has decided to give chase. As can be seen, the Forty-one-footer is steered with the help of a steering wheel much like that on a bus. The throttle is controlled by two hand-operated levers, one for each engine.

Previous page
The picture on the previous page was photographed under conditions that should be avoided by anyone who is afraid to get the camera wet. Although both boat and wave look as if they are stationary in the shot, this is of course an illusion created by a shutter that was open for just four-hundredths of a second. In reality the Forty-one-footer is plowing through water at top speed, and its massive bow is rising and falling with the size of the waves, which were reported to be three to five feet that day. But this is an everyday occurrence for the crew members, who have experienced both eight-foot waves (which is the "comfortable" maximum of a Forty-one-footer) and fifteen-foot waves (which is rather *un*comfortable).

The photograph on this spread shows a Forty-one-footer at speed under considerably calmer sea conditions just off the Florida coast. Power for these rugged Coast Guard workhorses comes from two Cummins diesel engines, which produce 320 hp each. The maximum speed of 26 knots requires 2650 rpm, while the economical cruising speed of about 10 knots is reached at 1800 rpm. The range is 300 nautical miles. The crew consists of four, including the coxswain—the person who steers the boat—and an engineer responsible for the smooth operation of the power units. Each man carries his own survival gear. In addition, there is an assortment of flares on board, as well as a gurney that floats, and an inflatable raft. The Forty-one-footer is also equipped with an electronic navigational aid system as well as a Raytheon radar unit with a twelve-mile range.

Previous page
In the picture on the previous spread the Forty-one-footer has encountered a suspicious vessel—suspicious, if for no other reason than that it is sailing in the waters between Bimini and Miami. But apparently something else, perhaps something in the way the sailboat looks, has attracted the curiosity of law enforcement agents on previous occasions as well, for the vessel, according to its captain, has already been stopped seven times and boarded twice. Of course, this could very well be a clever fabrication, and after some polite questions about previous ports of call and present destination—all conversation is handled from an appropriate distance—yet another boarding is thought to be in order.

The scene in the photograph on this spread captures the Coast Guard law enforcement officers as they board the suspected vessel. The Forty-one-footer stays close to the other boat just long enough for the transfer to take place, then retreats—the move takes some smooth maneuvering. The first action is to obtain the ship's documents, which are handed to the coxswain, who of course has remained behind the wheel of his vessel. He in turn, via the radio, checks with operations center as to the validity of the papers. In the end, the documents check out, and a thorough search reveals no contraband. The Coast Guard officers return to their boat after some complimentary remarks about the excellent condition of the sailboat, which turns out to have been built by the captain himself—not every encounter is an unpleasant drama.

Previous pages
The Coast Guard is reinforcing its fleet of drug busters with state-of-the-art speedboats, like the one seen streaking across the unruly ocean in the picture on the previous spread. This particular unit—also seen flying high in the picture to the left—is a prototype loaner; half a dozen all-white units will have been delivered by the time this book goes to press. This new type of go-fast, which in Coast Guard vocabulary will be referred to as an FCI (Fast Coast Interceptor), is designed and manufactured in Miami by Tempest.

The photograph above shows the captain at the controls. His left hand has a steady grip on the wheel, while his right hand keeps the two throttle levers close to their ultimate position. The speedometer shows 46 knots. Top speed under ideal conditions is said to be in excess of 50 knots. The length of the sleek Fiberglas hull is an impressive 44 ft. Power comes from two Caterpillar diesels, each producing 375 hp. These fast and powerful boats have been obtained for the explicit purpose of chasing drug smugglers. The waters in south Florida will soon be even more unsafe for every go-fast with illegal intent.

Previous page
The photograph on the previous spread illustrates yet another direction the Coast Guard is taking in its efforts to create effective drug busters. It is basically a Hurricane speedboat with inflatable rubber sides and vee-shaped keel, which has been modified by the knowledgeable folks at Base Miami Beach. The picture shows the three-man crew on patrol in the coastal waters just off Miami. The scene above gives an idea of the wake thrown by the twin outboard ONC engines, which produce 115 hp each, and a top speed of 55 mph.

The Hurricane, which measures 24 ft in length, is extremely sea worthy. Even though it will be primarily used in coastal waters, it handles itself with remarkable stability in rough seas, as is evidenced by the picture to the right, which was photographed in the inlet to Government's Cut, where the flow of the tide always makes for a bumpy ride. The Hurricane carries enough fuel—110 gallons, to be exact—to enable it to stay at sea for as long as twelve hours.

Back-ups and wild-cards

Every fighting force needs not only the front-line superstars, but also the behind-the-scenes workhorses—the ones who do the dirty work, the cleanup, the lifting and carrying and moving. In the air branch of the Coast Guard, an organization that likes to be coordinated and streamlined, one will find that the now-outdated Sikorsky Seaguard helicopter still is put to good use, performing all kinds of support duties. The Coast Guard also has a number of giant C-130 transport planes. These are used when a significant number of men and equipment are needed for a large-scale rescue operation or a specific law enforcement mission. The C-130s are stationed in Clearwater, which is located on the west coast of Florida, near Tampa. Customs runs a curious and intriguing fleet of back-up aircraft, as well as a couple of wild-cards, to be thrown in for those special occasions.

Pictured here, a Huey helicopter of 1963 vintage at the Customs base in Homestead. This was a front-line fighter before the arrival of the Black Hawks, and is still proudly carrying its decorations from numerous marijuana busts. Power for the Bell-manufactured helicopter comes from a Lycoming turboshaft engine, producing 1,200 shp. The fuselage is 42 ft long, height 14 ft and main rotor diameter 48 ft. Weight is just over 5,000 lb. Having first seen action in Vietnam, before spending several years as a drug buster, this old Huey has had a full life indeed.

The scene in the picture on this spread was photographed from the cabin of the Huey helicopter operated by Customs. Its less-than-nerve-tingling mission this day was to locate and photograph the wreckage of a small plane that had been the object of a chase the previous night. The plane had disappeared from the radar screen somewhere above the shallow waters south of Miami. It was thought that the pilot might have dropped his load of contraband and ditched his craft rather than risk landing and apprehension. It did not take long before the Huey found the small plane upside-down in the water. There was no sign of the pilot. The photograph would be needed as evidence if the case ever came to court.

Next page
Shown on the next spread is a view of the Coast Guard helicopter replaced by the new Dolphin. It is the old twin-engine Sikorsky HH-52A Seaguard, introduced to Coast Guard service in 1963. For twenty years it served admirably, becoming known and appreciated as the "flying lifeboat" because of its amphibious capability. It could actually be set down at sea if wave action was not too acute, and perform rescue missions from that position. The Seaguard has a maximum speed of 110 knots, and a cruising speed of 80 knots. The weight is just over 8,000 lb. The nose cone contains a FLIR (Forward Looking Infra-Red Radar). The helicopter is now mainly used for transport of men and materiel, a task it is well suited for, with its voluminous belly and impressive payload capacity. The fuselage is 57 ft long, height 18 ft, main rotor diameter 62 ft. This Seaguard is based in Clearwater

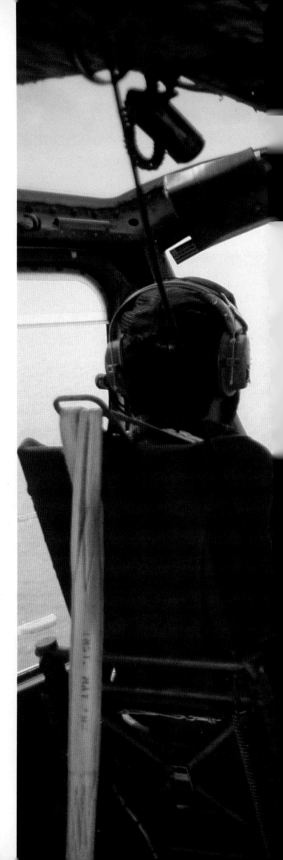

To the left, one of the wild-cards found in the backyard at the Homestead Customs base. This little Cessna 206 comes in handy for special occasions when an inconspicuous presence is required, as exemplified by a recent operation. The assignment required following—without arousing suspicion—a truck known to carry a load of contraband, as it made its way along the Florida Turnpike to its delivery point. The homely appearance of the Cessna, and its ability to fly at a slow speed, made it the perfect choice for the job.

Pictured above, another Cessna, this one a 1977 404 Titan. The plane once belonged to one of the bad guys, a Cuban drug smuggler, who spent thousands of dollars equipping it with all kinds of additional fuel tanks—there are auxiliary tanks in the nose and in the wings as well as in the baggage area—in order to turn the Titan into a formidable long-distance runner. The Cessna is capable of staying in the air for as long as sixteen hours without refueling. Confiscated some time ago, it seems a fitting twist of fate that it now serves the good guys.

Previous page
Captured just as it is getting ready to take off on another mission, the airplane in the picture on the previous spread is another of those curious Customs wild-cards—another of those innocent-looking drug busters. This is a 1957 Aero Commander, such a faithful old servant it has been given the nickname Emily. Emily is especially appreciated by the fixed-wing pilots in the Customs force for her ability to land and take off in very short distances, a feature that comes in handy when having to work from dirt roads and other make-shift locations. Barring the presence of electrical wires and other obstacles, she needs only about 600 ft for take-off. For landing, she can be brought to a complete stop after only half that distance.

The photograph on this spread shows the cockpit of the Aero Commander. The pilot, whose harness is not a seat belt but a shoulder holster, is on a routine reconnaissance mission over the ocean between Miami and Bimini. The high-wing configuration allows for an excellent view of the water below, and the power and speed—especially after turbo prop engines were installed—is quite impressive. Cruising speed is about 160 knots. Another aspect of Emily's flexibility is that, should it be necessary, she can fly as slow as 54 knots, using the flaps. Emily is, like the Cessna, a former drug hauler. She was confiscated and sold at an auction, whereafter she was again caught hauling drugs. This time Customs took her over for good, and she is now one of the veteran drug busters of the fleet.

The Customs pilots all use the standard-issue Army flight helmets, which seems to be the only concession to conformity—otherwise they wear equipment and clothing of their own choice. The only additional requirement is that they be armed—even here, there is a wide choice of options. Some pilots prefer a small revolver that can be worn inconspicuously in a hip holster, as in the photograph to the left, which shows a .38 Smith & Wesson Chiefs Special. The two clips hold twelve additional rounds of ammunition.

The photograph above further illustrates the relaxed dress code of the Customs pilots as well as their refreshing sense of humor. The T-shirt was specially designed for the purpose, and refers to the task of tracking and apprehending airborne smugglers in Bahamian airspace. The weapon is a twelve-gauge Remington 870 riot-type shotgun which, when not in use, is handily located in the corridor that leads to the helicopter pad. The magazine holds seven shots. An additional seven are kept in a holder fastened to the butt.

Moving into no-man's land

The long and varied Florida coastline, with its innumerable keys and islands, is indeed difficult territory to defend against the attacks of sinister invaders. And, to make things even more complicated, there is the Everglades, with its impenetrable marshlands and labyrinthian network of waterways. While the indigenous inhabitants of this Nature's inferno—the snakes and the alligators—undoubtedly think of this part of the world as a paradise, there is another species that long ago found it to be a haven as well—the drug smugglers. Here, perfect hiding places can be found, square mile after square mile of never-visited country, where contraband can be received from the air and where it can be stored with minimal risk of discovery. However, even this frontier has become less hospitable to the bad guys. Increased electronic surveillance has made air drops much riskier. And since Customs recently began outfitting the good guys with airboats, life for the smugglers promises to become increasingly unpleasant.

The photograph on this spread shows a rear view of one of the new airboats delivered to the Customs base located on Marco island. An aircraft propeller, powered by a 350 hp V-8 of General Motors manufacture, gives the boat a speed in excess of 50 mph. Although it feels a bit awkward to begin with, the airboat is easy to operate. There is no clutch and no brake—the only pedal is the one controlling the throttle.

Shown here, a Customs airboat at full speed. This special version is manufactured by Panther Airboats in Cocoa, Florida, and holds a crew of six. The operator and a passenger sit in the back seat, two occupants sit in the front seat, and one crew member sits on each side, by the railings on floor-mounted seats. Steering is actuated by moving a lever, which is connected with two rudders mounted immediately behind the propeller. Fuel is carried in two forty-gallon tanks. Exhaust from the engine runs through two tubes fitted with mufflers and exits through the stern of the boat, which is made of aluminum and has an absolutely smooth bottom. The airboat is not confined to the channels, but travels as easily across the grassy marshes.

On missions in the Everglades, where many rival smuggling organizations operate, it is important to show your colors. An intruder thought to be eyeing your stash can be shot without further ado, while most smugglers are wise enough not to mess with the authorities. In these pictures the Customs agents are wearing their regulation jackets, which are marked with appropriate badges and imprints. The agents are also well equipped when it comes to arms— above, the AR-15 assault rifle, made by Colt.

The agent in the picture to the right wears his .357 Smith & Wesson in a fast-draw type of spring-loaded shoulder holster which, when properly worn, stays more to the front than other kinds. The gun hangs with the muzzle pointing up, and the butt pointing down to the right. To draw, the agent just grabs the butt with the right hand and, pulling down and out, swings right onto the target in a fast and convenient motion.

Relics of peril in paradise

The Bahamian island of Bimini is the big-game fishing paradise first made famous by Hemingway in the thirties. Thanks to its close proximity to the Florida coast—by air it can be reached in less than half an hour—this island, and others in the vast archipelago, has in the eighties become the playground for another kind of adventurer, the drug smuggler. Contraband arrives aboard large fishing vessels or freighters—mother ships—that sail up through the Caribbean and transfer their load either to a depot on one of the many deserted islands and keys, or to smaller fishing vessels or go-fasts at sea. These then transport the goods to Florida. But the drugs are just as often brought in by air, in which case the contraband is landed onto small strips or dropped in the water. And since the strips are few and far between in this ocean paradise, the planes are simply ditched. With the astronomical worth of these loads, a plane, once its mission is completed, becomes an expendable asset.

If the plane sometimes is expendable, so too is the pilot. Since the activities described above usually take place during the hours of darkness, and the small airport on Bimini is both hard to find as well as unmanned and unlit, there are numerous wrecks to be found in the surrounding waters. This photograph shows the lone landing gear of a DC-3 that, after having overshot the strip, flipped over on its back as it hit the water. The rest of the plane lies buried in the sandy bottom. It is a lonely place to come to rest. A place mostly frequented by the pelicans.

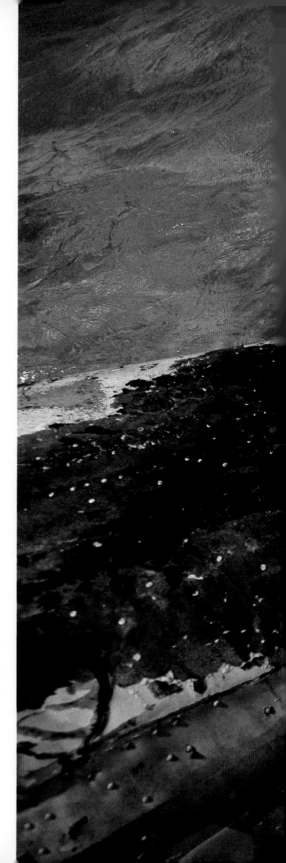

On the Atlantic side of Bimini, which is the unprotected side, the waves are more aggressive and their constant pounding more damaging than on the protected, lagoon side of the island. Here, as seen in the photograph on this page, the battered tail section of a small plane has been discovered in the shallow waters not far from land. Even though it seems to have crashed relatively recently, the sea has already begun its destruction, breaking open the fuselage and peeling off the paint. This plane, like the DC-3 on the previous spread, also seemed to have overshot the strip and flipped over when impacting the water. The engine had already been salvaged, but the instrument panel was still intact inside the cockpit, whose doors had been torn off, allowing the waves to wash in and out among the switches and gauges.

Next page
The scene on the next spread was found on the protected side of the island. Here the corrosive destruction is done by the strong tidal currents that flow continuously. When this picture was taken, the tide was at its lowest, revealing the misfortunes of yet another DC-3. The spot lies near the landing path, and the huge bird seems to have set down just moments too early. Errors of this kind are not just committed due to difficult navigational conditions, but just as often because the pilots are throwing good judgment overboard in their efforts to avoid detection and escape the pursuing planes of law enforcement authorities. The sight of the broken-off wing is indeed an eerie one, and a poignant reminder of the deadly game that is played out under the storybook skies of this island paradise.

COKE BUSTER

70

The people involved in the drug enforcement efforts are a tough and determined lot. The close-up photograph on this page focuses on the nose portion of one of the Black Hawk helicopters, with its small no-nonsense script, and serves to illustrate the certain pride these men and women take in their work. This is a war where the boundaries between good and right and evil and wrong are clearly defined. And what is good and right is always worth fighting for.